HOW TO DRAW
MONSTERS
AND OTHER SCARY STUFF

ARCTURUS

ARCTURUS

This edition published in 2015 by Arcturus Publishing Limited
26/27 Bickels Yard, 151–153 Bermondsey Street,
London SE1 3HA

Copyright © Arcturus Holdings Limited

ISBN: 978-1-78404-487-9
CH004419NT

Written by Paul Gamble & Anna Brett
Illustrated by Paul Gamble
Edited by Joe Harris, Anna Brett, Samantha Hilton & Frances Evans
This edition produced by JMS Books

Supplier 26, Date 0815, Print run 4547

Printed in China

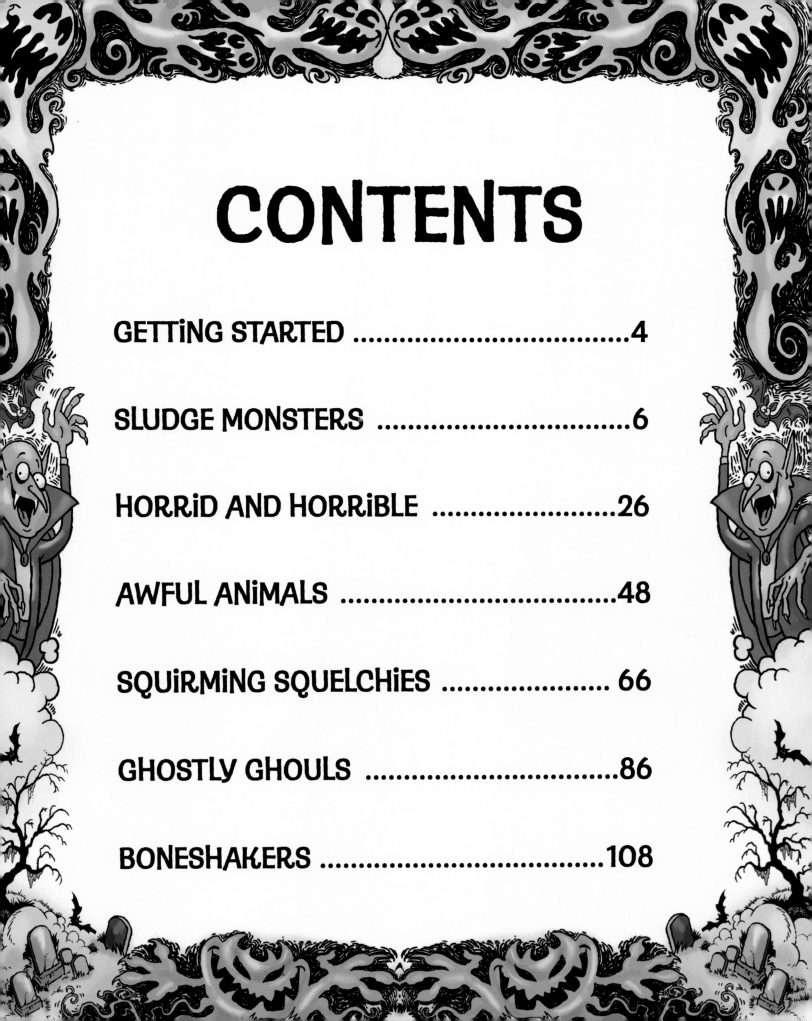

CONTENTS

GETTING STARTED

This book will teach you how to draw a cast of really horrible characters. Simply follow the step-by-step instructions and get drawing!

1. Start with a plain piece of unlined paper. If you are going to paint your picture, you should use thick paper.

2. Use a pencil to copy the step-by-step instructions. Soft pencils are good for rough sketches. Hard pencils are best for details.

3. Draw over your pencil lines with a black pen or a thin brush and black ink. The ink must be waterproof if you are going to use paint that is mixed with water to shade in the monsters.

INK

4

4. When the pen ink has dried, use a large, soft eraser to remove the pencil marks. Now your picture is looking nice and neat!

5. Complete your picture by shading it in with felt-tip pens, pencils, or paint.

6. Paintbrushes come in different shapes. When painting, use a thin, pointed brush for detail and a fatter brush to shade larger areas.

SLUDGE MONSTERS

Get ready to meet the terrifying four-eyed Ogglemonster and his horrible gobble gang!

ODDBALL

With three legs, this little monster hops around at top speed causing lots of mischief! He loves playing hide and surprise!

SLUDGER

Just one touch of Sludger's foul-smelling, toxic slime is enough to turn your skin green! He lives in a deep, dark swamp.

SQUIDRIP
Mind you don't get caught in these tentacles! Once Squidrip gets hold of something, he won't let go... unless you tickle him, of course!

GROSS GREMLIN
Don't let his cute face fool you. This monster has some horrible habits. Picking his nose, farting, and burping are the things he loves best!

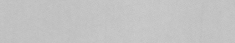

GOB MONSTER
Gob just can't keep his giant jaws shut and is always spraying spit all over the place! Don't ask him to say any terrible tongue-twisters!

OGGLEMONSTER

1. Ogglemonster starts life as a rectangle with a slight wobble to it.

2. Add two triangle-shaped ears to the top of the body. An arch separates his two legs.

3. One, two, three, four eyes and a mouth! Erase any original guide lines you no longer need.

4. Give Ogglemonster some arms. One curves up, the other curves down. Maybe he's doing a dance?

5. Add two toothy tusks and some fingers. Not so friendly anymore!

6. Now for the finishing touches. Add some claws, boils, pupils, and some gooey mud! Fill him in with a bright shade of red or orange.

9

ODDBALL

1. To start Oddball, draw a slightly squashed circle with a squiggly tail.

2. Add curved lines where his horns and three legs are going to be.

3. Draw in Oddball's stinky feet and pointed horns, and add arms. Give him a nice tail, too.

4. Draw in the rest of his legs, and add his first eye. Did you notice that Oddball only has two toes on each foot?

5. Give him fingers and two more eyes. Add the warts on his tail, and draw his open mouth.

6. Fill in his mouth, and add pupils and small movement lines around his body. Shade him in using purple and orange for his body and horns.

SLUDGER

1. To create Sludger's shape, draw three squashed circles overlapping each other.

2. Start his horrible face with eyeballs and a large mouth. Add lines and ovals for his arms.

3. Use the eyebrows to make him look mean. Make his arms look big and strong, and add hands, too.

4. Draw in his deadly slime bucket and the fingers on his left hand. Add pupils to his savage stare!

5. Finish drawing the bucket and his hands. Now let's add some slime!

6. Fill in his mouth and eyes, then go slime crazy! Make him as gloopy and horrible as you can! Finally, shade him green and make his bucket brown.

GOB MONSTER

1. Start drawing Gob by placing one small oval above a larger one.

2. Connect the ovals with some curved lines to create Gob's huge mouth. Then add some big eyeballs.

3. Gob's lower lip is huge! Draw a nice big rectangle for it.

4. Erase any guide lines you don't need, and connect Gob's mouth and lip. Draw the outlines of his hands and feet, and add an "X" for his tie.

5. Mark where his hair will be. Add in pupils and a floppy tongue. Draw his goofy teeth, fingers, and toes.

6. To finish Gob, tidy up your lines, and shade inside his massive mouth. Then fill him in using bright green and fluorescent pink. Don't forget to add that horrible flying spit!

SQUIDRIP

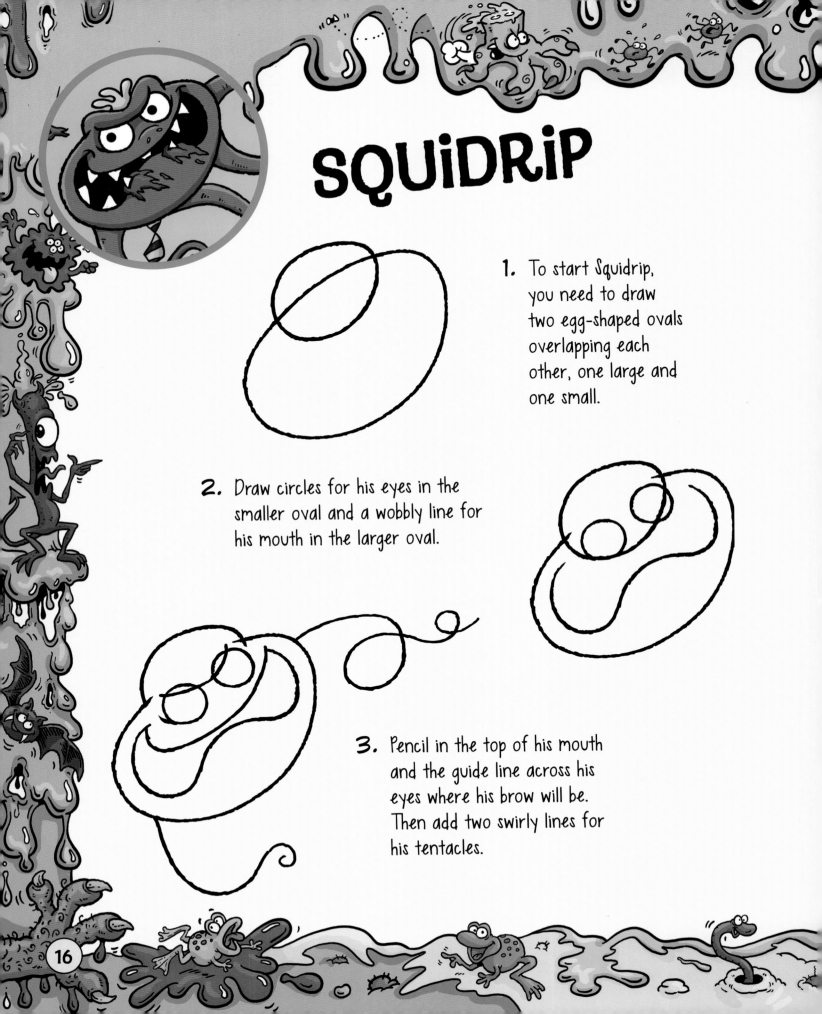

1. To start Squidrip, you need to draw two egg-shaped ovals overlapping each other, one large and one small.

2. Draw circles for his eyes in the smaller oval and a wobbly line for his mouth in the larger oval.

3. Pencil in the top of his mouth and the guide line across his eyes where his brow will be. Then add two swirly lines for his tentacles.

4. Squidrip has four tentacles. You can doodle any shape or swirl to start them.

5. Finish the tentacles. Give him pupils and teeth, then mark where his school tie will be.

6. Shade in his mouth, and don't forget to add the shreds of material caught on his teeth. He's just taken a bite out of something!

GROSS GREMLIN

1. Our tiny friend, Gross Gremlin, starts out as a pear shape topped with a squashed circle.

2. Draw the outlines of his hands and feet. Be careful with the positioning, since we're drawing him side-on.

3. Erase any guide lines. Then give him pointed ears and draw in his little arms.

4. Draw his legs, toes, fingers, and horns. Put a big curved line in where his mouth will be. He looks pretty cute at the moment!

5. Add fluff to his ears, then give him eyes and teeth. He's not so cute now that he's picking his nose!

6. Now to finish him. Make his outline furry, draw in his tie, and shade him in!

MUD FiGHT!

Use your pencils and felt-tips to finish this scene! Can you spot the unhappy hand?

HORRID & HORRIBLE

Meet Mini Mummy and other horrors from the world of the living... and the dead! They're out to wreak havoc!

FEARSOME PHARAOH
He used to be the King of Egypt, but now he's the King of the Dead! Beware his stare and avoid his tomb of doom.

MR BONES
You'd better hope that this scary skeleton isn't lurking in your closet, ready to rattle his bones at you. In life he was a history teacher, now he's history!

SNEEZY LUIGI

When Luigi sneezes it's like a fireworks display. High-speed green snot rockets out of his nose every few minutes!

VOMITING VICTOR

Ever since he was dared to eat some frogs' legs, Victor has become a human vomit fountain! No one knows when he'll stop, or who will clear up the trail of slop!

ZACHARY

Poor baby Zachary is covered with horrible itchy boils and scabs. The pox is just part of the problem, though, as Zachary catches every illness going!

MiNi MUMMY

1. Start Mini Mummy by drawing a large circle and then adding a small rectangle for his body.

2. Draw two small circles where the hands will be and then two ovals for the feet.

3. Sketch in his arms and Mini Mummy begins to take shape. You can add the open mouth now, too.

4. Flesh out the arms and legs, adding four fingers. Then work on his evil face.

5. Add some pupils and gappy teeth. Then start to draw lines where his bandages are.

6. Finish Mini Mummy by filling in his eyes and mouth in black. Draw the rest of his bandages, and leave two small holes for his nose. Give him green eyes and a red tongue.

FEARSOME PHARAOH

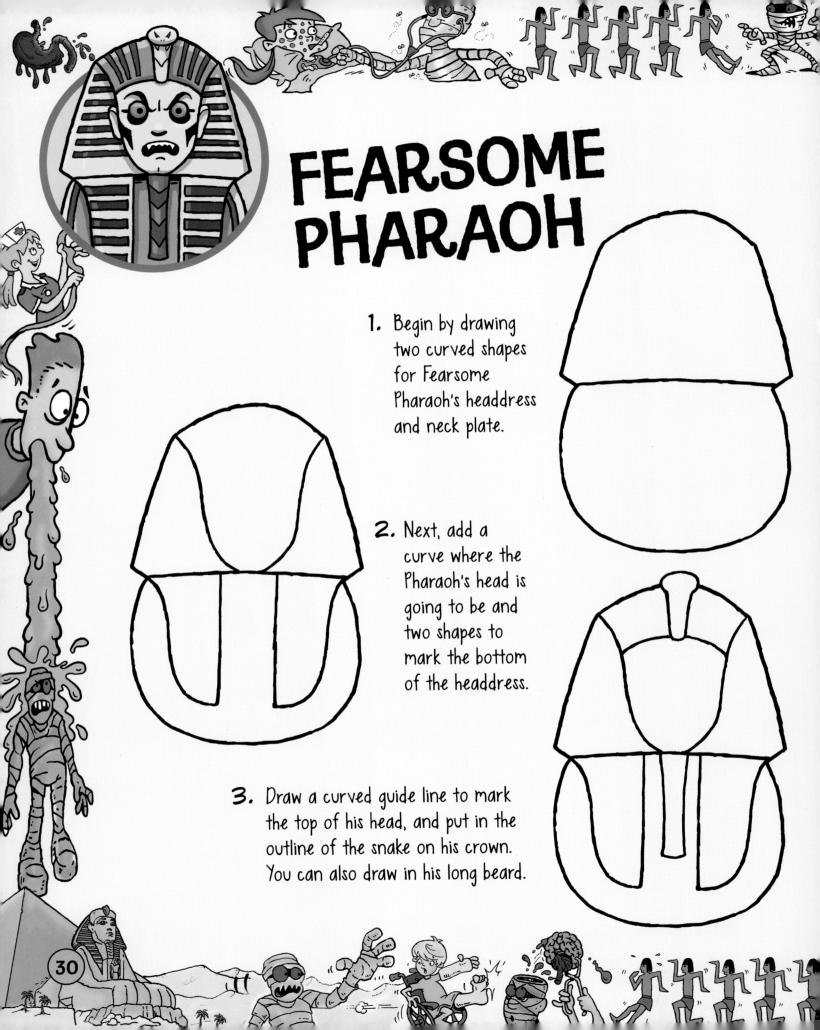

1. Begin by drawing two curved shapes for Fearsome Pharaoh's headdress and neck plate.

2. Next, add a curve where the Pharaoh's head is going to be and two shapes to mark the bottom of the headdress.

3. Draw a curved guide line to mark the top of his head, and put in the outline of the snake on his crown. You can also draw in his long beard.

4. Add two lines around the bottom of the neck plate, then give Fearsome Pharaoh his ears, eyes, and mouth. Add in the sneering snake's eyes and nose.

5. Add the stripes on the headdress, and braid the beard. Give him big eyebrows, eyeliner, fangs, and markings on his cheeks.

6. Add pupils, a furrowed brow, and some shading to finish your majestic portrait. Paint it in regal gold and royal blue!

MR BONES

1. Start Mr Bones by drawing a semicircle where his head will be, plus two kidney shapes for his ribs and hips.

2. Add in his triangular jaw and bones for the top of his arms and legs. Draw the classic bone shape a few times to get it right.

3. Draw in the rest of the arms and legs, paying attention to his pose. Then draw small rectangles where his spine will be.

4. Mr Bones does not enjoy being dead, so give him angry eyes! Add small shapes for all his joints.

5. Draw pupils and a mouth. Then add fingers, toes, ribs, and splits in his arm and leg bones.

6. Add the finishing touches to Mr Bones as shown in the picture, and you're done. He's chasing all those pupils who haven't done their history homework!

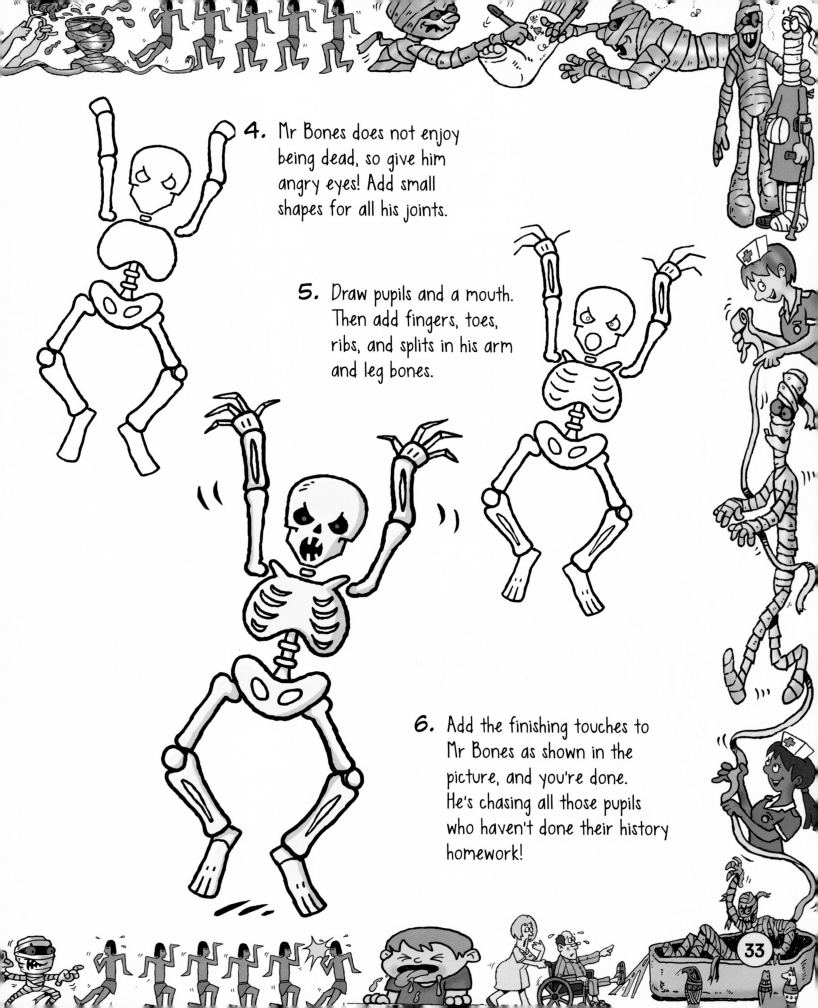

VOMITING VICTOR

1. Before Victor starts vomiting, he begins life as a soft-cornered rectangle connected to a curved body shape.

2. Add another curved shape for his legs, and then two circles where his hands will be.

3. Draw the outline of his open mouth, his left arm, the fingers on his left hand, and his feet.

4. Finish his fingers and add eyeballs and legs. Then draw the stream of vomit; it's as thick as one of his legs!

5. Make a nice puddle of vomit on the floor. Yuck! Then draw a nose, hair, and some large bags under Victor's eyes.

6. Give Victor some pupils and eyebrows, then shade him in. Make his vomit as horrible as you can! Why not draw in what he ate for his last meal!

SNEEZY LUIGI

1. Draw a circle, then attach the rectangular shape of Luigi's torso to it.

2. Draw the outline of his bent legs, his tissue, and a circle where his hand is going to be.

3. Add some arms and feet. He has bent legs to show the force of his sneeze!

4. Divide his legs in two, then give him some fingers and an ear. Outline his T-shirt, hair, and tissue.

5. Add in some more detail to the T-shirt and his hair, then draw triangles for your snot guide lines!

6. Finally, add extra wrinkles around Luigi's eyes to show they're squeezed shut. Don't forget to fill in his clothes. Then choose a gruesome green for the flying snot!

ZACHARY

1. Start by drawing a triangle with a circle sitting on top. This will help you get Zachary's proportions right.

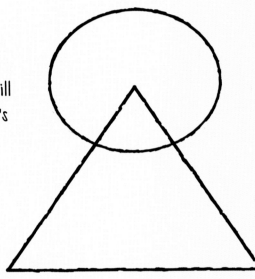

2. Within the triangle, draw an egg for the body, beans for the feet, and sausages for the arms. Feeling hungry?

3. Add circles where his hands will be. Then add legs and a big, wailing mouth.

4. Erase the triangle guide lines. Now he's taking shape. Draw fingers, ears, closed eyes, one big tooth, and a tongue.

5. Time to add detail! Add buttons and cuffs to his outfit, then concentrate on his face.

6. To finish your angry baby, give him lots of nasty pimples all over his face. Then shade in his clothes and choose a bright pink pencil for his mouth and spots. Tears and movement lines show Zachary is really grumpy!

SOMETHING HAS FRiGHTENED THiS TREASURE HUNTER. DRAW WHAT HE CAN SEE iNSiDE THE PYRAMiD.

43

Fill up the page with your own rotting mummies. Don't forget to add some brains and other organs!

AWFUL ANIMALS

Look out for Crunchy the Croc and a whole host of other nasty beasts in the awful animal kingdom!

CRUSHER

Crusher loves to catch people in his coils and squeeze them to death! He loves to eat chunky monkeys.

STiNGER
The last thing anybody wants is a cuddle from Stinger. Once he wraps his stinging tentacles around you, there is no escape from the pain!

MR PiNCH
He may be small but watch out for those pincers! Mr Pinch can snap bones in half with his powerful claws.

BRUTUS
Lightning quick, with razor sharp teeth and jaws that could crush a cow, it's no wonder that Brutus is the terror of the seas!

CRUNCHY THE CROC

1. First, draw a semicircle, which will form the base of Crunchy the Croc's body.

2. Draw the outline of his head and a bean shape for the start of his tail. It doesn't look much like Crunchy yet...

3. Next, pencil in those snappy jaws. Draw the tip of his tail and four circles where his feet are going to be.

4. Time to draw in his legs and connect his tail. Erase the guide lines inside his mouth, then outline his eyes.

5. Crunchy needs angry eyebrows and claws to look scary. He's taking shape now!

6. Finish Crunchy with lots of spikes down his back and pointed teeth. Most crocs are green, but you can make Crunchy any shade you like!

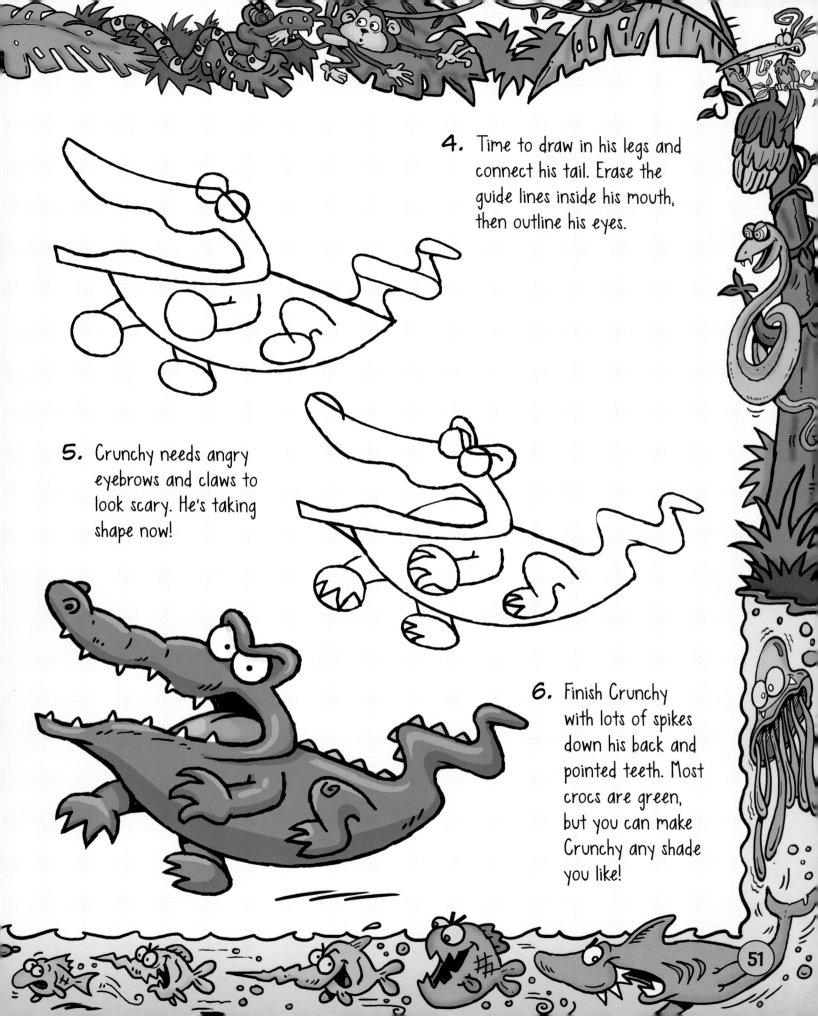

CRUSHER

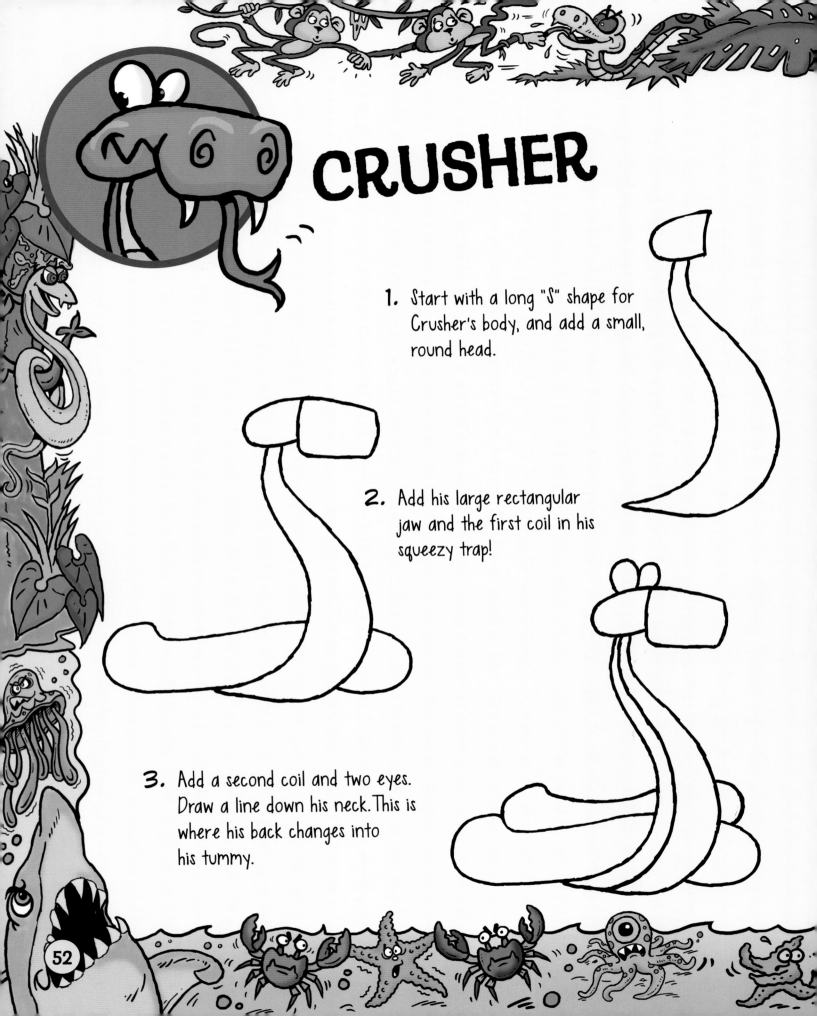

1. Start with a long "S" shape for Crusher's body, and add a small, round head.

2. Add his large rectangular jaw and the first coil in his squeezy trap!

3. Add a second coil and two eyes. Draw a line down his neck. This is where his back changes into his tummy.

4. Add a third coil and a wavy tongue. Add a circle to show where the monkey's hand is going to poke out.

5. Draw the final coil and finish the forked tongue. Now add the four-fingered monkey hand.

6. To finish Crusher, choose some bright pencils to shade him in, then give him pupils, nostrils, and fangs. Draw lines across his tummy, and he's ready to eat his dinner!

MR PiNCH

1. Begin to sketch Mr Pinch by drawing an oval leaf shape.

2. Draw two more leaf shapes above the first one. These will be the pincers.

3. Add some arms to connect the pincers to the body, two eyes, and the tops of his legs. It looks like he is doing ballet!

4. Make the bottoms of his legs pointy, and then create his big pincers by drawing a lightning shape across the oval.

5. Thick eyebrows, shadows under his eyes, and a creepy smile turn him from a regular crab into a cunning crustacean!

6. Mr Pinch is almost ready. Just choose some eye-catching paints to fill him in. Then add a single tooth and pupils, and he is ready to scuttle off... sideways, of course!

BRUTUS

1. To draw Crunchy Croc's pal Brutus, start off with a fat banana shape.

2. Draw a line down the middle to show where his belly will be, put a fin on his back, and start the tail.

3. Add his smaller fins, and mark where his gaping mouth is going to be. The tail is a quarter-moon shape.

4. Draw in an eye and some gills. This is the last time Brutus is going to look friendly.

5. Give him angry eyes, pointy teeth, and show where his tail has a battle scar from a fish fight.

6. To finish Brutus, fill him in, then shade the inside of his mouth and around his eye, for an extra evil glare!

STINGER

1. Start off with a curved semicircle. This will be Stinger's large head.

2. Draw a squiggly frill across the bottom, and add two round eyes.

3. Add the beginnings of the six tentacles. Make them wavy, like hair.

4. Finish drawing the thick tentacles, and then draw a long, smiley mouth.

5. Time for the horrible part! Give him some fangs and heavy eyelids.

6. Finish Stinger with purple pencils, then add shading, pupils, spots, and bubbles to show that he's underwater.

Fill in the **OCTO-LAIR,** then see if you can find a starfish with a ring and the fish with a light.

SQUIRMING SQUELCHIES

Harry Hornet and the squirming squelchy gang will eat anything... rotten food, smelly stuff, and even human toenails!

RAVENOUS RUTH
Ruth has twenty legs and a long body to fill with food, so she's always got her fork at the ready for the next snack.

GUZZLETUM
The fattest, meanest, greenest frog in the swamp, he lurks behind the lilies, pouncing on unsuspecting flies, and belches after every mouthful!

SQUiRMY WORM
Squirmy's a crafty chap. He wriggles around, in and out of the ground, dodging birds and hoarding all the best food for himself!

SQUELCH
This naughty spider is named after the noise he makes. He loves it when he bites into his prey and it goes SQUELCH! There's no escape once you're caught in his web.

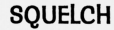

SNOTTY SNAiL
You can always spot where Snotty Snail has been because he leaves a sticky, green trail behind him. Don't touch it, though, or you'll get stuck!

HARRY HORNET

1. Harry Hornet has an oval-shaped body. The fatter end will be his head, so decide what direction you want him to face.

2. Add two wings on top of his body, and notice how the back one goes behind the body. Add his pointed stinger and nose.

3. Draw in a huge eye and a zigzag line for his mouth. You can erase the guide lines across his wings and nose now.

4. Connect Harry's nose to his mouth, and add in the second eye. Draw curved lines around his body for markings.

5. Time to add some details: eyebrows, the open mouth, and lines on his wings. A puff of air behind him shows he's flying.

6. Finish your artwork by painting in the stripes with black and yellow, then add some veins to Harry's buzzing wings.

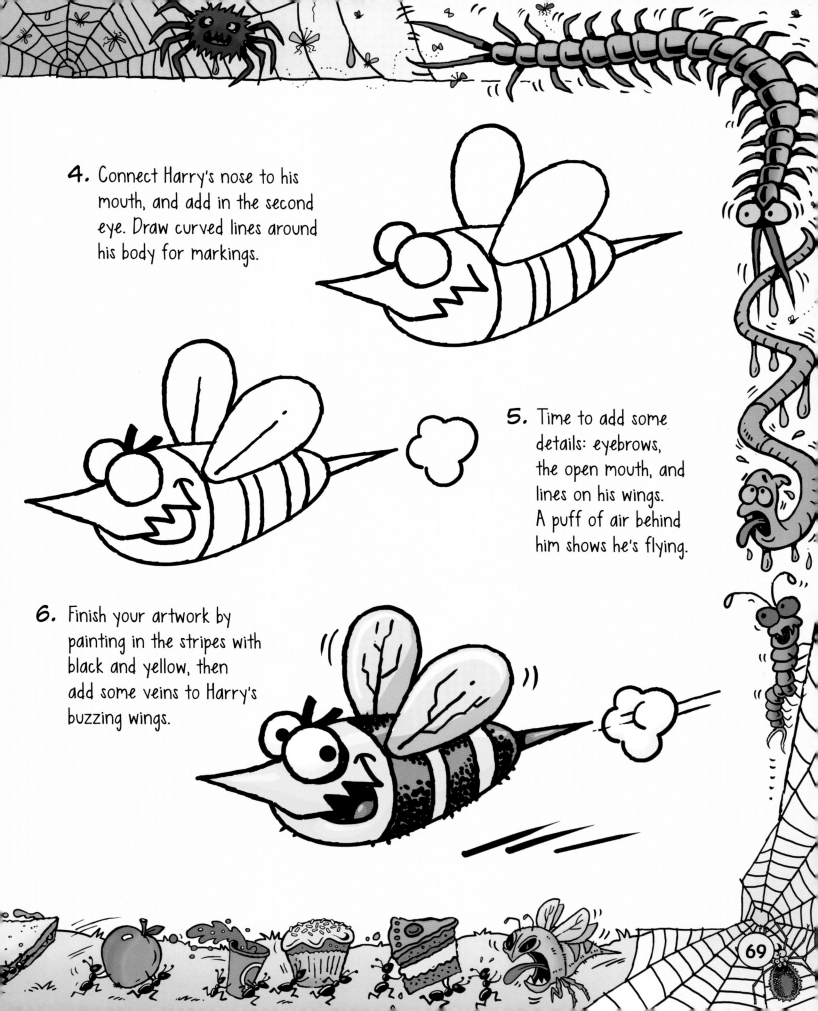

RAVENOUS RUTH

1. This hungry caterpillar starts out as an oval at the end of a squiggly line. She looks like a tadpole at the moment!

2. Begin to build up her body by drawing lots of ovals stacked on top of each other.

3. Continue drawing ovals until you have a total of ten. Then add some googly eyeballs. Now she's starting to look like a caterpillar!

4. Draw some patches on each segment of her body, and add arms and a smile. Erase any guide lines.

5. To make her truly weird, add hair everywhere, goofy teeth, and a long tongue.

6. Finish her by adding her feet, pupils, and antennae. With a fork in her hand, she's ready for a meal! Use different felt-tip pens to shade in each part of her body, and choose bright pink for her tongue.

SNOTTY SNAIL

1. Make the basic shape of Snotty Snail's body by drawing a triangle with wavy sides.

2. Draw the round head and long tail at either end. He looks like a slug without his shell!

3. Now add a soft square shape for Snotty Snail's shell, and then draw his eyes floating above his head.

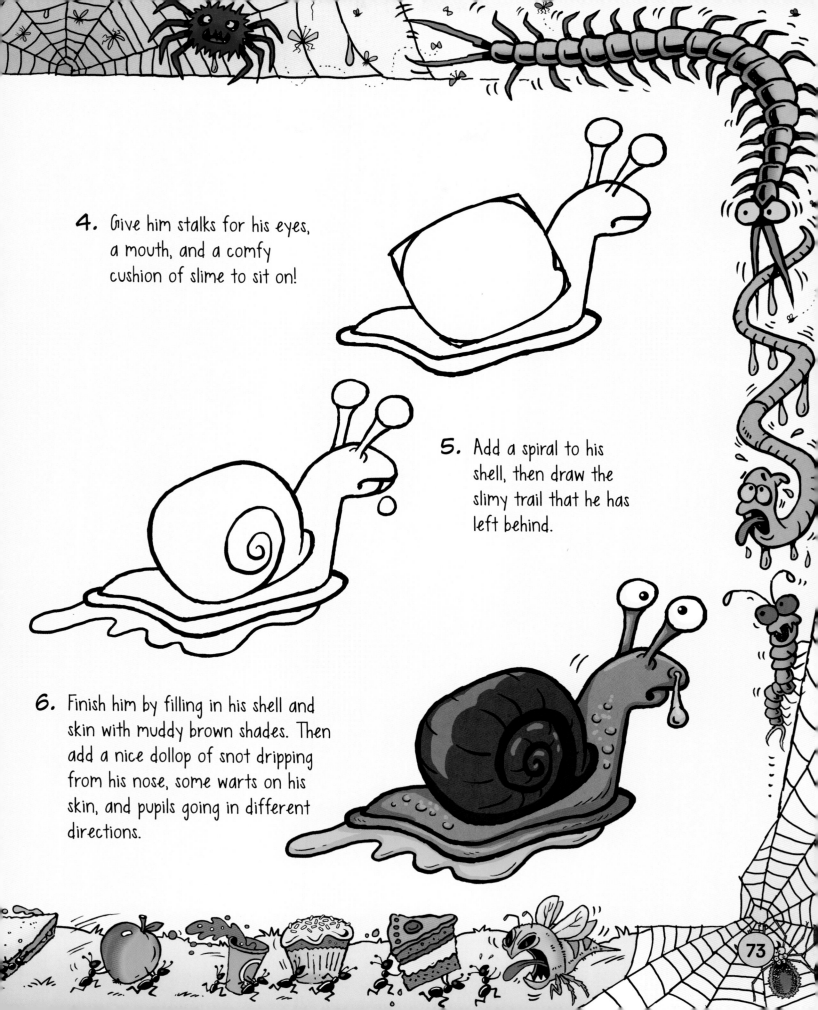

4. Give him stalks for his eyes, a mouth, and a comfy cushion of slime to sit on!

5. Add a spiral to his shell, then draw the slimy trail that he has left behind.

6. Finish him by filling in his shell and skin with muddy brown shades. Then add a nice dollop of snot dripping from his nose, some warts on his skin, and pupils going in different directions.

SQUIRMY WORM

1. Squirmy begins life as two sausage shapes next to each other.

2. Add two more smaller sausages above and below your original shapes. Give them slightly pointed ends.

3. Now connect the ends of the four sausages to form a wriggling body. Try changing the angles to create a different pose for Squirmy.

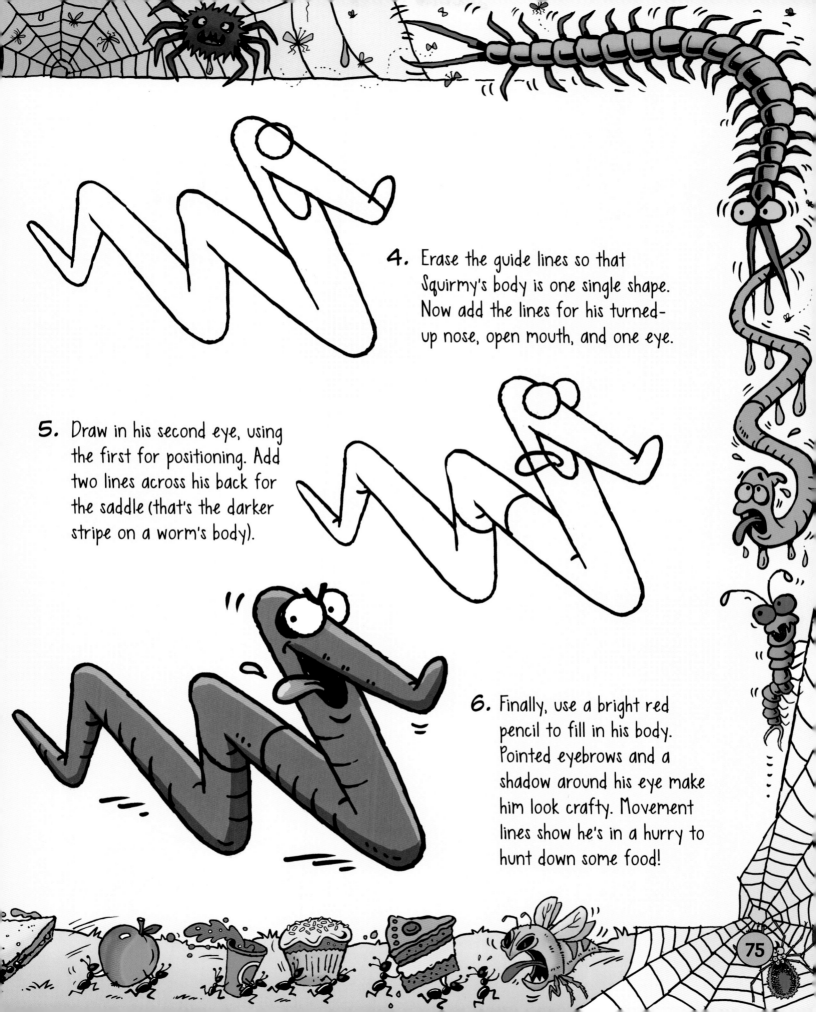

4. Erase the guide lines so that Squirmy's body is one single shape. Now add the lines for his turned-up nose, open mouth, and one eye.

5. Draw in his second eye, using the first for positioning. Add two lines across his back for the saddle (that's the darker stripe on a worm's body).

6. Finally, use a bright red pencil to fill in his body. Pointed eyebrows and a shadow around his eye make him look crafty. Movement lines show he's in a hurry to hunt down some food!

SQUELCH

1. Start with an easy circle for Squelch's body. How large are you going to draw him?

2. Add eight lines sticking out of the circle for his legs. Count to make sure you've got them all.

3. Now make the legs rounded and add two eyeballs. Spiders actually have eight eyes, so you could add another six to your drawing!

4. Time to transform him into the naughty spider he really is! Give him angry eyebrows and a wide mouth. Draw in a jagged line around his body.

5. A furry body and fangs make this a spider to steer clear of. Outline his tongue, too.

6. To finish Squelch, give him pupils and shade around his eyes. Add some hairs on his legs, then shade him black, blue, green, or purple.

GUZZLETUM

1. To begin drawing this frog, sketch a circle, then put a sausage shape on top of it.

2. Draw arches for the outlines of his back legs and triangles for his two front feet.

3. Draw wide triangles for his back feet, and add three toes on each front foot. Add two eyes, and then show where his giant mouth is going to hang. Make it huge!

4. Add toes on the back feet and then shape his mouth. I wonder how many flies he has swallowed today?

5. Now draw his long, sticky tongue flying out to catch prey. Give him some angry eyebrows, too.

6. Finish Guzzletum by adding lots of warts and his pupils. Then shade him in with green and bright pink for his tongue. Don't forget to finish off the poor fly!

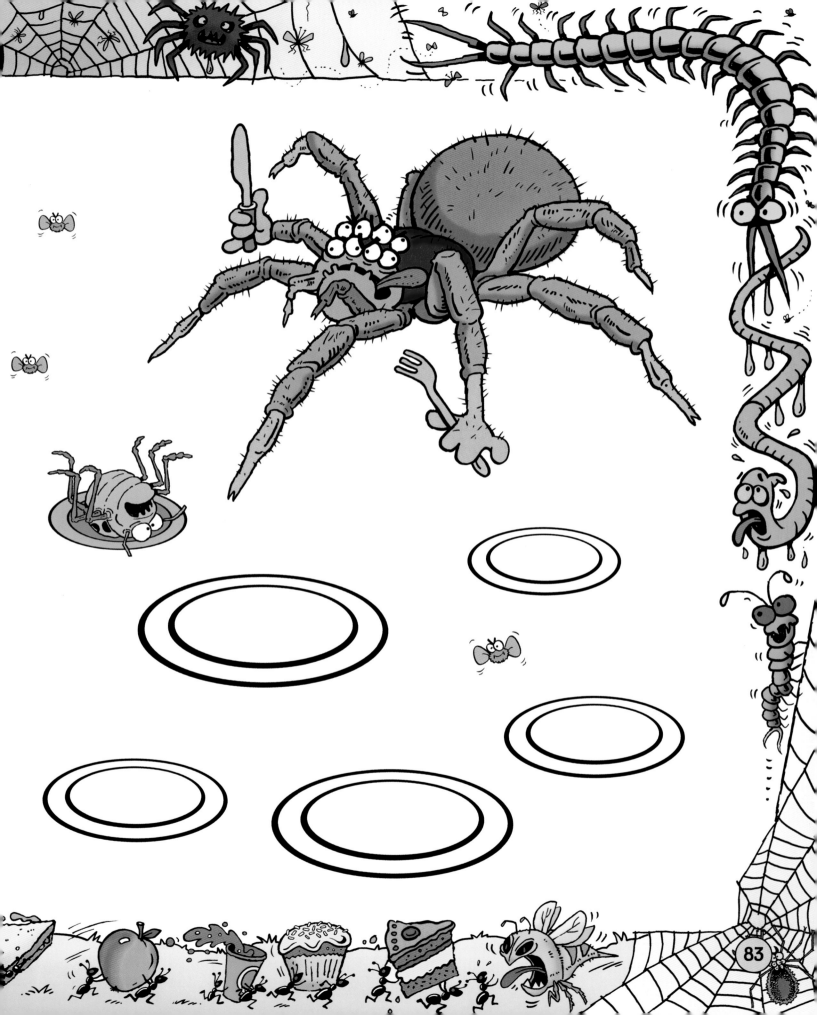

GHOSTLY GHOULS

This gang of ghouls is led by Vampella. Her teeth are the sharpest in the business.

BLACK WING
This guy is Vampella's right-hand bat. He's got an amazing sense of smell, so needs to avoid flying into Zombie Zeke!

ZOMBIE ZEKE
Zeke's stench is enough to make you puke! He's an expert at the zombie shuffle, especially with his decaying limbs.

WILD WANDA

Wanda is as ugly on the inside as she is on the outside. Beware her broth, it'll turn your face green and your nails black!

SID THE SPIRIT

This mischievous spirit is out to have fun. He's top of the shocks and loves to spook little kids and puppy dogs.

DRACO JUNIOR

Don't be fooled by Draco's good looks, he's the most feared creature of the night... and has a very famous father!

VAMPELLA

1. To draw Vampella, start with a circle connected to a long bell shape.

2. Add carrot shapes for her feet and circles for her hands. She has pointed, pixie ears.

3. Sketch in the outline of Vampella's long hair, then add her arms and legs.

4. Draw her wicked, pointy fingers, and make the bottom of her dress ragged. She's been wearing it for over 200 years!

5. Finish her flowing hair to show she's flying, and don't forget those fearsome fangs.

6. Add dark shadows under her eyes and sloping eyebrows to give her a crafty look. Give her a blood-red dress and green skin. Vamp-tastic!

DRACO JUNIOR

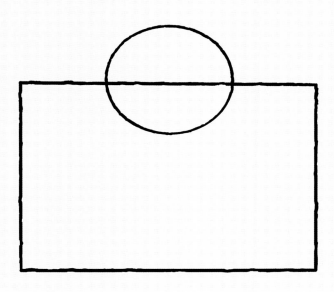

1. Draco Junior's no square, he's shaped like a rectangle! Add a circle at the top for his head.

2. Draw a triangle for his body and two smaller circles for his hands.

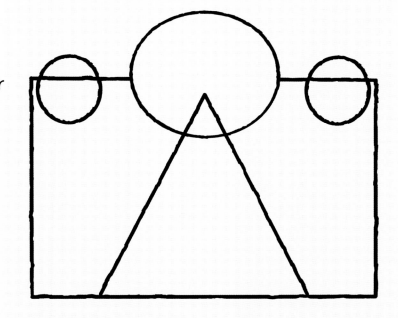

3. Two triangles look like ears, but they're really the top of his cape!

4. Time to add some eyes and give the bottom of the cape a batwing shape.

5. Now draw in his pointy ears and fingers, and add his cheeky face!

6. Finally, add fangs and finishing touches. Shade him in with purple, red, and black pencils.

SiD THE SPiRiT

1. Sid starts life as a curved rectangle. Easy!

2. His arms are up in the air and shaped like bananas. Spirits don't have legs, so make the bottom of the rectangle ragged.

3. Add circles for hands, a curve at the back of his head, and some more tatters at the bottom.

4. Sid's clawed hands make up for his lack of legs! Now's the time to add a wicked grin.

5. Give him evil eyes by drawing little semicircles. His jagged teeth are just mini triangles.

6. Sid's in fright mode, so add some movement lines around his body. Shade around his eyes and his jagged bottom. He is a creepy shade of green.

WiLD WANDA

1. Begin with a shape like a witch's hat. It's a triangle with a longer bottom.

2. Draw a circle inside the triangle, and add two pointy arms on either side.

3. Draw a circle around her head, a line for the bottom of her dress, and a "V" shape for the broom.

4. Get your eraser out, and suddenly Wanda begins to take shape. Draw in her feet, face, hands, and hair.

5. The tip of her hat is bent, a lot like her large nose! Draw it in, along with her eyelids and open mouth.

6. The finishing touches include lots of warts! She has a single tooth and wicked eyes. Her face and dress are green. Watch her fly into the night to cause mischief!

ZOMBIE ZEKE

1. A bell or a pear? This is how Zeke starts life. You could try to draw a whole zombie army.

2. Add a circle for the head and two ovals for his feet.

3. Draw a triangle between his feet to get the shape of his legs. Two circles will become his hands.

4. Add circles for his eyes, a bean-shaped mouth, tattered clothes, and zombie arms.

5. I don't think a dentist would be happy with Zeke's teeth, since even his floppy tongue is trying to avoid them!

6. Now add the details: pupils, shadows under his eyes, ragged clothes, and drops of slop! Shade him a sickly zombie blue.

BLACK WING

1. Black Wing begins life as a large triangle with a semicircle on top.

2. To get the shape of the wings, connect the ends of the semicircle with the edges of the triangle. The little circle will be his head.

3. Erase the top of the triangle, and add lines across the wings. Draw in his body.

4. You can draw in the full wing shape now. Add his pointy ears, too.

5. Time to add a face and erase all the guide lines you no longer need.

6. Finish the wings, and give him a furry body. Last but not least come his fangs. He is a vampire bat, after all! Shade him purple.

DRAW THE INGREDIENTS THAT HAVE GONE INTO THIS WITCH'S BROTH.

BROTH RECIPE

1 squeeze of slug's slime

4 spiders and their webs

1 chicken's foot

1 bat's wing

The bones of a wolf

10 newts' eyes

1 whole octopus

3 frogs' legs

WHO SPOOKED THE VAMPIRE SLAYER?

BONESHAKERS

Welcome to Dr Stitchup's crazy laboratory! Nothing will stop him in his quest to create an army of monsters!

iGOR
Every mad scientist needs a hunchbacked sidekick! They don't come more stupid than Igor, but he's handy for cleaning up blood and guts.

BONEHEAD

Bonehead has the most marvellous brain, which Dr S. is determined to preserve. He keeps him in a jar in his lab. Many of the most horrible experiments are Bonehead's idea.

CHICKENSTEIN

Created as a pet for Igor, Chickenstein wasn't too happy about having his wings replaced with hands. He's been in a bad mood ever since.

FRANKIE

This creation is Dr S.'s pride and joy. He was created out of dead patients and sewn together with bolts and screws. Watch out for his fiery temper!

DR STiTCHUP

1. Dr Stitchup has a body shaped like a bell. His head and neck are long and thin. Copy the odd shape!

2. Time to add arms and legs. If you start with a single guide line, it's easier to get the shape right. He's got bent legs and raised arms.

3. Now add six circles: two for the hands, two for the eyes, and then one for his ear and collar.

4. Finish the hands, and add a flask raised high in the air. All mad scientists need a pair of stupid specs and wild hair.

5. Even though this scientist is mad, he knows it's important to wear gloves when he's handling chemicals!

6. Finish his face with wild eyes, and make his hair frizzy. Use blue and orange pencils or paints for the rest of his outfit. Finally, add buttons to his lab coat.

BONEHEAD

1. Begin by outlining Bonehead's skull shape. He doesn't have a body, so you can make it nice and large.

2. Draw two round eyes and a triangle for his nose hole. His nose fell off many years ago!

3. Give him a large grin, and draw a line to divide the top of his skull. Notice the squiggly line next to his eye. This forms the side of his face.

4. Add stitches along the crack in the skull and some remaining teeth. Bonehead's sitting on a plate.

5. Erase the lines on the mouth, add a curve around the eye, then draw in the bell jar.

6. Finally, add the details: pupils, a black nose hole, and some shine on the glass of the jar. Then use glowing green and purple to fill him in. Bonehead's a medical marvel!

iGOR

1. Dr Stitchup's weird henchman, Igor, begins life as an egg shape.

2. Add the circle for his head within the body shape. This creates the hunchback. He has two little legs...

3. ... and feet shaped like beans. Add two round hands. Different-sized eyes help make him look stupid.

4. Add in the arms and legs. It looks like he's hopping! His big smile extends beyond his eyes.

5. Give him a big goofy tongue and some ears. Draw on the rags he wears.

6. To finish off, use some pencils or paints to shade him in. Igor's never been to the dentist, and he only has one tooth left.

CHICKENSTEIN

1. Igor's pet, Chickenstein, starts life as a triangle with curved corners.

2. Add an oval on the left and a semicircle on the right, then draw curves around them. Make sure you leave a big gap.

3. Two circles on the top of the triangle form his googly eyes. Add five fingers between the ovals and the curves to form his hand-wings!

4. You can erase the extra guide lines on his hand-wings now. Next, add a triangular beak and two short legs.

5. Fingernails and feet come next, then three circles for his comb.

6. To finish Chickenstein, use red and orange pencils or paints to shade him in. Stitches hold his hands in place, and a cloud of dust suggests he's on the run. Maybe he's trying to escape from the lab!

FRANKIE

1. Dr Stitchup makes his monsters from dead bodies, but all you'll need to make Frankie are some paper and a pencil. Start by drawing a wonky rectangle.

2. Add an egg shape for the right foot, a semicircle for the left foot, and a rectangle for the head.

3. Divide both the head and body rectangles in two. Add lines with large circles at the end for the arms and hands.

4. Create an arch between the two feet for Frankie's legs. Add fingers and eyes, and then start the bolts that hold his head in place.

5. Give Frankie some hair and a face. Finish the bolts and the tattered edge of his shirt.

6. Stitches show where his head was cut open to insert the brain. Use green and blue shades to fill him in. Pupils in different positions show he's only just come to life! Eureka!